SONG OF A DRIFTER
AND OTHER BALLADS

Also by Barry Crump

A Good Keen Man (1960)
Hang on a Minute Mate (1961)
One of Us (1962)
There and Back (1963)
Gulf (1964) – *now titled* Crocodile Country
Scrapwagon (1965)
The Odd Spot of Bother (1967)
No Reference Intended (1968)
Warm Beer and Other Stories (1969)
A Good Keen Girl (1970)
Bastards I have Met (1971)
Fred (1972)
Shorty (1980)
Puha Road (1982)
The Adventures of Sam Cash (1985)
Wild Pork and Watercress (1986)
Bedtime Yarns (1988)
Bullock Creek (1989)
The Life and Times of a Good Keen Man (1992)
Gold and Greenstone (1993)
Arty and the Fox (1994)
Forty Yarns and a Song (1995)
Crumpy's Campfire Companion (1996)
As the Saying Goes (1996)

SONG OF A DRIFTER

AND OTHER BALLADS

Barry Crump

Illustrated by
Pat Trembeth

The publishers wish to thank Maggie Crump and Hodder Moa Beckett for their help and co-operation over the publication of this book. Ballads published herein first appeared as follows: 'Song of a Drifter' in *The Life and Times of a Good Keen Man*, Barry Crump Associates, 1992; 'Journey', 'Time of Day', 'Cave', 'Battle', 'Harry's Piece of Pain' and 'Letter to the IRD' in *Bedtime Yarns*, Barry Crump Associates, 1988; and 'Fire' in *Crumpy's Campfire Companion*, Hodder Moa Beckett, 1996.

First published 1996

ISBN 1-877161-06-3

Published by
Hazard Press Limited,
P.O. Box 2151,
Christchurch, New Zealand

Cover painting by Dennis Kent
Illustrations by Pat Trembeth
Design by Quentin Wilson

Printed in New Zealand

CONTENTS

Quent, here's this lot.

It's a sorry mess and Maggie and I apologise for its presentation to you. However, we know that the pearl resides in the rough shell of the oyster.

This material is belated and we've worked all night to get the poems done. Use this material as you wish and pay us a just royalty on any of it you choose to publish and in whatever order you choose to put it. There's no need to consult us about editing or anything, we leave that to you unless you need our help.

Whatever else that needs consultation could probably be done on the phone, but if we end up in Christchurch or you have occasion to come up here we'd be delighted to see you.

At a quarter to six in the morning, 27 June 1996,

With fondest regards

Crumpy and Maggie Barry Crump

Introduction

This book recalls a voice that none of us will ever forget. Dry, sly, laconic and with the gravelly crackle of a concrete mixer. If you have any trouble with the tricky metre of some of these lines, try saying them aloud, and you'll catch the echo of Crump himself, and get the swing of them.

For Crump's words belong to an age-long folk tradition of ballads and songs, and his use of these forms is authentic. There is no false note in his lines and rhymes. They mean what they say, and they catch exactly the way he spoke and figured things out, the way he meant his writing to communicate and to be instantly approachable, though ever with the bald and banal messages you'd find on a placard.

There's nothing scrubbed and tidy and ironed about the way he wrote. His phrases were functional certainly, and they work, but you'll always find twists and convolutions and creases in his manner of putting things, and occasionally he also lets you see the rips and mends and stains.

Read 'Cave', for instance, and you'll find that dark and almost gothic side to his imagination, which every now and again, throughout his writing, shadowed his marvellous sense of fun, absurdity and adventure.

Or read 'Time of Day' and you'll discover a nostalgic

observer of the passing moment that lingers forever – in this case a 'moment of sadness' that wafts through his thoughts as he takes in the view of a wild river valley and becomes aware of the high-tension wires of the power pylons that cross it.

Yet here Crump makes his point without feeling the need to spell out an obvious remark about the way we treat our environment. He's not writing signs on a banner. The poet in him simply draws our attention to 'that mournful note in the cry of the putangitangi' (paradise duck) – that's all. And that's what makes the poem so effective.

Of course, when it comes to out-and-out satire – in 'Ode to a Politician' or in 'Letter to the I.R.D.' – Crump takes deliberate aim and hits his target. It all comes down to a question of sorting out your intentions and getting your tone and objectives right.

Crump was the greatest literary entertainer of his generation. Reading these poems makes one realise how much we all lost when he died on the third of July, 1996. There's not just the pleasure of the whole box of tricks they represent, but the joy of their sheer sparkle and gusto. The only regret I have is that he started to write in this style so late. At his best, he's as good as Banjo Paterson – and he's a lot more relevant to us. He would have become one of the best of modern balladeers.

It's a privilege to recommend to all readers this unguessed side to his talents, but it's also more than that. In 1963 Crump wrote an introduction to my first book of poems, and saw to it that they got published – in Christchurch, as it turned out. And now, thirty-three years later, it's my turn to write an introduction to his first book of adult poems – also published in Christchurch.

I can almost catch my old friend's marvellous voice in the distance remarking that it's funny the way things turn out, isn't it? And I've no doubt he's raising a glass to add that there are very few straight lines in life, are there? Everything bloody goes in circles.

KEVIN IRELAND
AUCKLAND, 1996

Mustering Bullock Creek

We'd mustered all of Doubleburn
And then within a week
A bloke called Jim had roped me in
To go and muster Bullock Creek.

He told me where the station was
And warned me it was steep,
Said he'd meet me there on Monday
At the homestead, Bullock Creek.

I'd seen some country in my time
From the North to Mitre Peak
But nothing like the mighty bluffs
They've got out there on Bullock Creek.

Gorges, cliffs and shingle-slides
To seven thousand feet
I knew I was a fool to try
And muster that there Bullock Creek.

The boss-man was a widow
And I signed on for a week
And she was tough, she had to be
To live four years on Bullock Creek.

It rained and we got flooded-in,
They phoned a message through,
The bloke called Jim had turned it in
And taken off to Timaru.

My dogs and I we had a go
We climbed up on the peaks,
Among the cloud and ice and snow
That never goes from Bullock Creek.

I risked my life a dozen times
And brought in sixteen sheep,
I can't forget that awful climb
My first day mustering Bullock Creek.

For three weeks there we risked our necks
To get four hundred sheep.
My dogs and I were nervous wrecks
From mustering on Bullock Creek.

My huntaway slid off a bluff
The rest were thin and weak
Those dogs were tough but they'd had enough
Of them there hills on Bullock Creek.

I got my cheque and hit the track
And man I'm never going back
I still see gorges in my sleep
From when I mustered Bullock Creek.

Toyota

Toyota in the Sheraton
Toyota in the mud
Toyota on the motorway
Or churning through the flood.

Toyota in the sandhills
Toyota in the town
Toyota parked in Dargaville
With people hanging round.

Toyota for a pack-horse
Toyota for a leap
Toyota for the open road
When everyone's asleep.

Listening to a western tape
The headlights on the line
We want to make the Ferry
And she sails at half past nine.

With a deer across the bull-bar
And a live one on the back
We boot her through the lupin
And make ourselves a track.

Toyota towing Henry's truck
Or humming through the Haast,
Looking for a camping-place
We knew of in the past.

Free of spares and spanners
On easy roads and rough
I spin my new Toyota
From the North Cape to the Bluff.

Ode to a Politician

You claim to lead,
You're in the rear,
So where the hell
Do we go from here?

You take from us
As though you could
In this way do
Yourself some good.

This old folks' home
Please tell us why
Our aged are thrown
Out here to die.

The old man eating
Hand-out stew
Once saw his comrades
Die for you.

Ask that woman
What she did,
You'll find that she
Raised seven kids.

The mental patient
Sent away
Had with joy that very day
Her baby by the motorway.

My eyes can see
Your policy
Your words don't mean
A thing to me.

It's time, my friend,
For worthy deeds,
Homes and jobs
Are what we need.

Your record isn't good
my friend
But soon now
Your career will end.

And one day you'll be asked
To say
What you did when
You had your day.

If you would start
To earn my vote,
Give that old drunk
Your overcoat.

Journey

The hand that felled and split the tree
And sank the posts in sand and scree
And strung the wire and battened-up,
Now raps the saucer with the cup.

The arm that slung the hauler-spragg
And sprung the breech and strung the stag
And swung the jangling ploughing-team,
Now reaches out to play the queen.

The eye that heard the southwind roar
And smash the vessel on the shore
And heard the names of shipmates read,
Now hardly hears what's being said.

The foot that trod the frozen clay
And kicked the winning goal that day,
The foot that once wore hide and steel,
Now puts its slippers on by feel.

The soul that since before its birth,
Now weary of its term on earth
And quickened by a glimpse of light,
Rejoices, and prepares for flight.

Time of Day

At that time of day
when the world turns away from the sun
and the last traces of sunlight
are gone from the ridgetops,
I lead my old horse down a wild river valley
with two trout in the split sack
behind the saddle.

Around the bend I see great wires
strung swooping from pylon to pylon
across the sky.

And I wonder how come
it makes that moment of sadness
waft through my thoughts,
and puts that mournful note
in the cry of the putangitangi.

Cave

Bushed and beat and too far back,
Raining hard and off the track,
Where's the road now – hard to tell –
Take a guess and go like hell.

Over the side of a dirty bluff,
Stuck on a ledge and no way off,
Round this shoulder – real close shave –
And here in the cliff is a hidden cave.

Dry sticks lying on the floor
And looking round there's plenty more,
And further back among the stones
A row of moulding human bones.

Bones and hair, things of the grave,
I've stumbled on a burial cave.
Outside the thunder rips the air
And I'm not going anywhere.

I light a fire, forget the storm,
And pretty soon I'm dry and warm.
But though he's weary from the chase
My dog just doesn't like this place.

I call him in, he sniffs around
But just can't seem to settle down.
His hackles rise, he growls again
And disappears out in the rain.

I must have slept an hour or so
When sounds of voices, soft and low,
Awake me from my stony bed –
And leave me staring at the dead.

People from beyond the grave,
Vague and smoky, fill the cave,
Crouched and mumbling, hairy-thighed,
Man and woman, squat and wide.

They speak in wary undertones,
A language that I've never known,
As though they might be overheard
If one should say a noisy word.

I see one as the flames leap higher,
Drag something smoking from the fire,
The carcase of some slaughtered beast –
And now they all fall on the feast.

They tear the steaming ribs apart,
One gets the liver, one the heart,
And soon the whole voracious band
Is dripping blood from chin and hand.

A hairy shoulder moves aside,
I catch a glimpse of what has died,
And with a chill that rips my spine
I see the dog they eat is mine.

Aghast and overcome with shock
I try to burrow in the rock.
The best thing I can do is crawl
To deeper dark along the wall.

And as I cringe in mortal fear
A savage bellow rends the air.
A hairy bull-man fills the door
Behind him there are many more.

They fall amongst the feasting clan
And club them senseless to a man.
Hacking, snarling, wood and bone,
Until their grisly work is done.

The floor is puddled flowing red
All the feasters lie there dead.
The victors, as they make to go,
Lay all the bodies in a row.

And as they leave one hairy brute
Looks round and sees me crouching mute.
He lifts his club with angry eye
I have to make a move or die.

I leap up with a desperate groan
And strike my head on jutting stone.
A flash of stars and nothing more –
I fall down on the cavern floor.

I wake, the dawn light fills the air
And find the bones, still lying there,
And every skull, the daylight shows,
Is cracked and split by heavy blows.

I leave that place, I find the track,
For sure I won't be going back.
A dream's a dream, but that was weird,
And now my dog has disappeared.

If someone asks I'll have to say
He sprouted wings and flew away,
'Cause who'd believe that poor old Ben
Was et by prehistoric men?

Battle

With trembling hand I undertake
To rectify a grave mistake –
Of certain academic flaws
In versions of the 'Maori Wars'.

I haven't lightly undertook
Correction of a history book,
But snugly rests the head at night
That has that day put someone right.

According to these gentlemen
There's only one thing for it,
A Maori couldn't comprehend
A good thing when he saw it.

I don't know what they seek to gain
By making this suggestion,
The soundness of the Maori brain
Has never been in question.

What fool would turn a bargain down
Like fish-hooks, blankets and an axe,
When all he'd known were wood and bone
And all he'd ever worn was flax?

What maniac would fail to swap
Some land for mutton, beef and hog,
When hitherto his only chop
Was bird, or rat, or skinny dog?

Who'd fail, unless he'd lost his wits,
To emulate the wily ones
Who sailed the world in mighty ships
And brought him tomahawks and guns?

And having got these wondrous things,
Who wouldn't want to try them out?
And that's what all the quarrelling
And all the fighting was about.

Any mother anywhere
Will understand the claim:
Give little boys the best of toys –
They'll quarrel just the same.

BRITISH GOVT.
IOU - NZ.
W.D + H.O. WILLS

And as the flag of God unfurled,
The different tribes across the world
In deadly clashes such as this,
Attacked each other's prejudice.

In spite of who believes they're right,
Or what men say they're fighting for,
The only kind of war we fight
Is still the same old human war.

So in the broader sense, you see,
The 'Maori Wars' will cease to be,
And future books will only say
That humankind grew up this way.

Letter to the I.R.D.

Dear Sir,
Your letter says – my conscience burns! –
I've never furnished tax returns.
And, furthermore, you seem to say,
It's getting too late anyway.

And, further-furthermore, you add,
The situation's very bad,
And if I don't, by yesterday,
Produce returns – there's hell to pay!

No problem, sir, we'll put that right,
I'll write it down this very night.
Employers, dates, in each detail –
We'll sort this whole thing out by mail!

You see, I've kept a careful track
Of everything, for income-tack,
And saved it for this very day.
Coincidental, sir? – I'll say!

So with respect for you and me,
I won't put on false modesty,
I'll just stick down the simple fax
Of you and me, and income tax.

I left home, sir at an early age
And went in search of work and wage
And got a job repairing sacks,
So I could pay some income-tax.

I didn't know that from the start
The firm was shaky – fell apart –
And by the time I'd paid the boss,
I stood a quite substantial loss.

I learned to cook and did so well
They made me chef at Brent's Hotel.
The fat caught fire, the pub burnt down
And, broke, I had to leave the town.

At trading I was doing well,
I couldn't get enough to sell.
My profits vanished – every cent –
The victim of embezzlement.

I then moved on to other things,
To seek the revenue they brings,
But one by one my ventures failed
And constant losses were entailed.

For instance in the timber trade
I really thought I had it made,
Until they went and 'sent me through',
To cheat the Inland Revenue!

You know yourself how these things are –
I had some trouble with my car
Then mortgage people haunted me
And drove me into bankruptcy.

And so the years have drifted by,
Regardless of how hard I try
(You might just call it rotten luck)
I haven't made a single buck.

But I didn't need to stay at school
To get damn good at mini-pool
Or learn that life gives nothing free,
It's what you make it, you and me.

Take me, now, who'd have ever guessed
I'd end too poor to invest
In things like inland revenue –
I think it's rather sad, don't you?

But when it comes to golf, old chap,
I'm on a seven handicap
And, yes, (How sharp of you to guess!)
I play a decent game of chess.

I know what won the Melbourne Cup
And what's the score in Bangladup.
I'll rattle off the All-Black Team
And tell you what it should have been.

I know the current price of gold
And just what shares were bought and sold;
I've heard the joke you'll tell tonight –
I guess you'd say I'm pretty bright.

But when it comes to currency
The blasted stuff just dodges me.
I tell you, sir, I've had a lash
At handling everything but cash!

fastpost
COMMISIONER FOR TAXATION
DEPT. OF INLAND REVENUE
PRIVATE BAG
CHRISTCHURCH
FINAL DEMA

And so, my friend, my point is made,
I give these details unafraid.
And when you come to judge my case
You'll feel the same as me, Your Grace.

But please don't think it's been in vain –
I know I'll soon come right again,
For after all it isn't *who*,
It's *what* you know that gets you through.

And meantime, sir, may I suggest
A way to meet the problem best –
Relying on our mutual trust,
You pay the tax for both of us.

And then when things come right for me
I'll do the same for you, you see?
It's one of nature's basic laws –
You pay my tax – I'll pay yours!

And one day, when I'm all cashed up,
I'll come to town and look you up.
No, really sir – I can't be rude,
I'll *have* to show my gratitude.

And when we're back to square again
And everything's as right as rain,
We'll have the whole thing sorted out
And no, sir, it'll be *my* shout.

And won't we chuckle when we see
How close we've grown, sir, you and me.
The bonds of friendship, forged on facts
Of you and me, and income-tax!

Just one last thing before I go.
You'll understand, Your Grace, I know.
I wouldn't need a large amount,
Let's just say fifty, on account.

The going's been a little tough,
But fifty bucks should be enough,
(A money-order telegram?)
I can't say, sir, how pleased I am!

And any time you need advice,
Just call on me, sir, don't think twice.
I wouldn't put you crook, you'll see –
We'll be good mates, sir, you and me!

I trust you, sir, no need to say
You'll send the fifty right away.
Don't worry, sir, you'll get it back,
See ya, cobber,
Your Friend,
Jack.

Bad Blue

I got a dog off a bloke who was passing through
For a retread tyre and a beer or two,
Its name and breeding no one knew,
It was black and tan and I called him Blue – just Blue.

I took him home and, blast his hide,
He sank his teeth in my backside,
My trousers tore like a rotten sack,
I guess it doesn't pay to turn your back on Blue – not Blue.

I went out hunting and I took this blue
Just to see what he could really do,
And he rounded on an old boar pig,
Mean and lean and twice as big – as Blue.

He ran that boar down a razor-back
And bailed him hard on a greasy track,
They flattened fifty yards of scrub,
They wouldn't believe me in the pub – about Blue.

Blue latched on to a nine-point stag
And it shook him out like a sleeping-bag,
That stag put on a mighty show
But he couldn't make that Blue let go – not Blue.

He shook the fleas off Blue's old hide
And dragged him down a shingle-slide.
He trampled Blue till his knees were weak
And tried to drown him in the creek – that Blue.

The stag gave up in sheer despair
And Blue hung on till I got there.
Killed that stag with my skinning-knife,
Best dog I had in all my life – that Blue.

Within a week I was in the gun
For all the damage he had done,
My wife she left me in despair
She wouldn't stay while Blue was there – not Blue.

He lost an ear and he lost an eye,
I lost count of the scars on Blue's old hide.
He slipped his collar in my sleep
And killed eleven Romney sheep – Bad Blue.

Blue didn't die from poison-baits
Or rifle shots or bitten mates,
He didn't die from wounds or weather,
He ate my fowls and died of feathers – Poor Blue.

If there's a heaven where the good dogs go
I reckon Blue's been sent below,
And I'd like to see the sparks that flew
When the Devil turned his back on Blue – Bad Blue.

Cup of Tea

Sitting with my sister and a milky cup of tea,
Talking chat of this and that, a thought comes over me.
I suddenly remember some of how I've spent my time,
And I see a few occasions where I've wandered out of line.

Life at home among the family saw me oft across the knee,
And some of that, I reckon, could have been because of me.
And I must have been a nuisance to the teachers at the schools,
It might have turned out better if I'd understood the rules.

The lies I told the ladies, the ones I told in court,
Were mainly only borrowed from the things that I'd been taught.
And other bits of mischief that crop up inside my head –
Perhaps the only reason is because I'm easy-led.

I could put it down to ignorance and maybe ease my mind,
But I could have given Peter more than twenty bucks that time.
I can't remember what I've lost, or had ripped-off from me,
But I can't forget those boots I stole when I was twenty-three.

Though it's not the indiscretions of the past that bug me now,
It's the ones I keep repeating that still bother me somehow.
I know, as years go tumbling by, we'll all come right at last,
But have I got sufficient years to tidy up my past?

I see the things I need to change, how simple it all seems,
Such little things have kept me from fulfilling all my dreams,
But then this thought is very shy, a timid reverie –
I blink away the whole display, my sister says, 'More tea?'

Fire

O Fire, what message
Have you imparted
To my vacant mind
As I stared those thousand hours
At your gesticulating flames?

What wisdom have you whispered
To my unguarded ear
In your snapple and crack
And your muttering blaze?

Is the talk of Tawa wiser
Than the Rata or the Gum?
Is the sparkle of the Totara
More profound than either one?

Or are you just returning
Your substance to the sun,
And I just use its burning
On your smoking journey home?

O my servant, my companion,
Cook my food and warm my bed,
Dry my clothes and keep me cosy,
Keep me safe and keep me fed.

And yet I've heard fierce wars being fought
In the hunger of your conflagration
And see Tyrannosaurus Rex wink at me
From the embers of your grave.

Harry's Piece of Pain

Harry Roper found a bench and rested in the sun,
Studying his fellow man at shuffle, walk and run.
And as he watched with lidded gaze the bustle and the din
All the voices died away but the one that said, 'Come in.'

'Come in' it said. And then again, 'Come in' he heard it say,
And though he waited patiently it wouldn't go away.
And then he saw a passing crowd move out across a plain
Unable to resist the voice, 'Come in' it said again.

He saw a shining mountain there, a door was open wide,
He saw the people shed their cares and start to move inside.
And very soon a multitude was flowing in and past
And Harry knew that humankind was coming home at last.

Everyone who ever lived, from everywhere on earth
Was heading for that mighty door, regardless of their worth.
From every long and latitude, from every tribe they came,
And everyone who entered there was greeted by their name.

And as they passed within the door the lame were made to walk,
The blind were made to see again, the dumb were made to talk.
The guilty left their fear outside like rows of muddy boots,
And very soon the plain was strewn with faulty attributes.

The rich were made to shed the load they'd carried all their lives,
The parted were united with their husbands and their wives.
The poor were lifted from the road they'd trodden all their days,
The heedless lifted up their eyes in gratitude and praise.

Humble, worn and sick at heart, and weary of the fight,
They heard the voice that said 'Come in,' and hurried to the light.
And when at last they'd all gone in and left him on the plain,
He gazed around the empty world and hung his head in shame.

He saw across an oily sea great smears of greed and gain,
And on the other side was loss and want and pain.
All the ignorance of man was there to see, and yet
The only thing that Harry felt was sadness and regret.

And now he hadn't any choice, no time to lose or win,
He had to turn and face the voice that said once more 'Come in',
And as he moved toward the door he wept, because he'd seen
A better life he could have lived – the way it should have been.

They found old Harry sitting there, a dribble on his chin,
They put him in a wooden box and said a prayer for him.
They lowered him in the ground, the place from whence he'd come.
They stood and thought, the score of life? When added up, what sum?

Song of a Drifter

I've cut me load, and that's me song,
It's time I hit the track,
I've been round here for far too long
And now I'm headin' back.

I'm splittin' from this worn-out scene,
I'm packin' up me gear,
I'm takin' off for pastures green,
I'm snatchin' it from here.

I've heard the things they said to me,
I've bogged meself in stuff,
I've took responsibility
And now I've had enough.

I'll drag me hook, I'll just un-front,
I'm headin' for the door,
I'm castin' off, I'll pole me punt,
I'm not here any more.

So good luck, mate, I'm movin' on,
I'll leave the place to you,
And if they ask you where I've gone
Just tell them I shot through.

And if we meet some other place
A stranger you will be,
I can't remember name or face,
They're all the same to me.

I'll greet you like a brother;
I'll make you laugh somehow,
And then one day I'll drift away,
Just like I'm doin' now.

PAT TREMPET
THE HUT IN THE DONALD